BOA
EDITIONS LTD

NOMINA

NOMINA

Sonnets by
KAREN VOLKMAN

American Poets Continuum Series, No. 109

BOA Editions, Ltd. ❊ Rochester, NY ❊ 2008

PS
3572
.O3547
N66
2008

First Edition
08 09 10 11 7 6 5 4 3 2 1

For information about permission to reuse any material from this book
please contact The Permissions Company at www.permissionscompany.
com or e-mail permdude@eclipse.net.

Publications and programs by BOA Editions, Ltd.—a not-for-profit corporation
under section 501 (c) (3) of the United States Internal Revenue Code—are made
possible with the assistance of grants from the Literature Program of the New
York State Council on the Arts; the Literature Program of the National Endow-
ment for the Arts; the County of Monroe, NY; the Lannan Foundation for support
of the Lannan Translations Selection Series; the Sonia Raiziss Giop Charitable
Foundation; the Mary S. Mulligan Charitable Trust; the Rochester Area Com-
munity Foundation; the Arts & Cultural Council for Greater Rochester; the Stee-
ple-Jack Fund; the Ames-Amzalak Memorial Trust in memory of Henry Ames,
Semon Amzalak and Dan Amzalak; and contributions from many individuals
nationwide. See Colophon on page 72 for special individual acknowledgments.

Cover Design: Steve Smock
Cover Art: Luca Buvoli © 2006. Detail from *Propaganda Poster–And I Used to
    Close My Eyes (Triple-Blue Shadow), with Protovector with Painted "Y,"* 37 x 30 x
    3 inches. Gouache and pencil on monoprint, wood frame, glass, metal, enamel,
    and polyurethane resin. Courtesy of the artist.
Interior Design and Composition: Richard Foerster
Manufacturing: Thomson-Shore
BOA Logo: Mirko

Library of Congress Cataloging-in-Publication Data

Volkman, Karen.　# 173248 991
  Nomina : sonnets / Karen Volkman.
    p. cm. — (American poets continuum series ; no. 109)
  ISBN 978-1-934414-06-4 (pbk. : alk. paper) — ISBN 978-1-934414-07-1 (alk.
paper) 124626
  I. Title.

PS3572.O3947N66 2008
811'.54—dc22
                                    2007039117

BOA Editions, Ltd.
Nora A. Jones, Executive Director/Publisher
Thom Ward, Editor/Production
Peter Conners, Editor/Marketing
A. Poulin, Jr., Founder (1938–1996)
250 North Goodman Street, Suite 306
Rochester, NY 14607
www.boaeditions.org

NATIONAL
ENDOWMENT
FOR THE ARTS

State of the Arts

NYSCA

Contents

II

She knows that the more the events traverse the entire, depthless extension,
the more they affect bodies which they cut and bruise.

As the dream a consciousness adored
beached its semblance in a mist, a mere
oval emulates a circle, austere
lack, swart spiral. Opacities are poured

in midnight ciphers, alembic of the shored
remnant, naufrage the hours cannot steer
north of founder, and ruin is the clear
attar on the tongue, trajectory of toward

blue as blindness in the ocean's stare.
Oh the minus when it runed and roared.
Lucid cumulus (the wind's white hair),

indignant plural of the single word,
rages, retrogrades. Omega air
all formless fire, a body of the lord.

Brown is the flat gestation of a maze,
grass-grown remembrance of a second look
the field holds open like a nascent book
in which the wind has written, Sudden strays,

sudden numbers beat—the roots of days
branched intangibles a stupor took
and slept and stroked and scattered in a shook
haze of wakenings, refracting rays

outleaping their seasons, daughters of a glance
ago-ahead, a retrograde advance.
Loving nothing but the fractal ways,

they gather flowers—pearl-petal, bitter blaze—
brilliant sisters in the infinite dance
at ardor's axis, integral of chance.

Sweetest bleeding is the cipher of sleep.
Soundless loaming, burying its dead.
The raw rilled lexicon that no one read.
No word survives the color of this deep,

this black unsinging—the wave escapes the leap,
its edges flatten—a syllable, a said
spell like pearl an ocean bore and bled
dying in harrows. Palliative, a sweep

blacks and satins. Sad sirens burn and sigh,
caressing the umber inner of a thigh—
unfolding in the flimmer of their hair

the swimming timbre, the wakeful stare
loosens its wooings, and wakes to die
drowning mutely, hollow as the sky.

The sky we bear on our shoulders, heaven-height
and livid firmament, delineated dream
sounding distance, when distant spaces seem
silence, absence, unconsummated sight.

Atlas-Argus. Hard burden, dim delight
to bear, to blur, to peer, to stitch the scheme
opposing wind to figure, bright supreme
mind colluding in all that nascent night.

Lidded Argus, bent Atlas—caught between
world-scar, mind-ire, exigencies that blind
and hobble-harrow, double-dwindle, delete

heaven-quotient, exceeding heaven's mean.
The pain divisions. And x, the coldest mind,
skies the sentence, articulate, complete.

Spring's portion, a sweet sifting.
Aggregate spirit, portent or part
a limbic tincture, textured heart
effacing the product of its lifting

white conduction in the bolus of a drifting,
as if. As of, apprised, apart,
it really was. It really hurt.
A game ago, a seismic shifting,

a few blocks back, blacked out. Broke in.
Backed off. Spoke more, in wish, said less.
Said this, sad such. Or some dumb grin

encrypted in the crude protection.
Abed a blue bent, dead bless,
the brutal of the person we'd have been.

Say sad. Say sun's a semblance of a bled
blanched intransigence, collecting rue
in ray-stains. Smirching pages. Takes its cue
from sateless stamens, flanging. Florid head

got no worries, waitless. Say you do. Say
photosynthesis. Light, water, airy bread.
What eats its source, its orbit? Something bad:
some plural petal that will not root or ray.

Sow stray. Salt night for saving, dreaming clay
for heap, for hefting. Originary ash
for stall and stilling. Say it *will*, it said.

Corolla corona, bliss-bane—delay
surge and sediment. Say instrument and gash
and ruminant remnant. Rex the ruse. Be dead.

Never got, and never thought, and yet
always potent in the never-been
the ever-urge to always arc, to spin
aim's injunction in a raw roulette

ever placing never's bankrupt bet,
carbon numbers, impossible to win
at null, at zero, an integral skin:
cardinal animal in an ordinal net.

What fury frauds the nod, what squalid set?
Base Ire, base Err, base *Bas*, the baseless bane
of never's radical, the swelling square

of pallid possibles that slip and stare;
unsummed digits, unformulated stain
ever's ardor will never not beget.

Coracle, rime, red ocean,
little barque that pilots so
drowsily your errant motion
nor waves' bright wake nor hollow—

adrift, spectacular liquor,
imperator of the divine,
each drop, nor core nor outer
the arc of other define –

to drown is frame or custom,
as water is ember or air
aspiring to livid fume,

firmament rained with sounds
the network swallow and scare
and the red little barque resounds.

Laughing below, the unimagined room
in unimagined mouths, a turning mood
speaking itself the way a fulling should
overspilling into something's dome,

some moment's edging over into bloom.
What is a happening but conscious cloud
seeking its edge in wound or word
pellucidity describing term

as boundary, body, violated bourne
no sounding center, circumscription turn.
Mother of mirrors, angel of the acts,

do all the sighing breathing clicking wilds
summon the same blue breadth the sense subtracts,
the star suborning in its ruptured fields.

It's nothing. A blue wheel blurring, and a wind
catchless, clicking at a window's high
startless framing—a fixed, transparent eye
that knows no solitude, and cannot spend

its stare on other spaces, never tend
those trees, that crooked keystone, this cold sky,
the cemetery with its stones and shy
flowers browning—a gaze without an end,

a silent keeper to the nothing news
stroking the surfaces of dreamless deeps.
And who can blame a blank that doesn't choose

or say the boundaries bound, the keeper keeps,
the law of glass is porous, the day we lose
greets the eye that blinds it. The other sleeps.

Sleeping sister of a farther sky,
dropped from zenith like a tender tone,
the lucid apex of a scale unknown
whose whitest whisper is an opaque cry

of measureless frequency, the spectral sigh
you breath, bright hydrogen and brighter zone
of fissured carbon, consummated moan
and ceaseless rapture of a brilliant why.

Will nothing wake you from your livid rest?
Essence of ether and astral stone
the stunned polarities your substance weaves

in one bright making, like a dream of leaves
in the tree's mind, summered. Or as a brooding bone
roots constellations in the body's nest.

Name your weapon. Wanton wink of lip,
or fraud of languor activates the ruse—
lofting litany or freighted fuse
ignites the slant, the stammer, and the slip,

mummery dumbshow, livid as a whip.
Egg or pupa, crush it where it cues
the baited future, tongue and scab and bruise
attached and hatching, spawning in the rip

needs and plangencies, and all is ill.
God of creatures, cripple what you kill,
engined, agented, the suckling spawn

replicated in the heaving mill.
Each breach is touch, each touch a flinch and spill.
Each urge a freak of need, a seeded yawn.

What are wounds for? Anticipants accrue
void to your harrow-vowel. Syllable
stammered and ordered, unitary will
deformed, divisible, consumptive blue

blotch is the gangrene weather! pall, ague
you atomize, cauterize—patient, shill . . .
Oh burn the blight. Just stanch it. Vatic pill
not noun, not *idem*—scarred flat phonemic hue

blinking its tinctures. Caligram we rue
and twine with veins. The sap seeps. Currents kill
the network, clockwork. Contingency's true

prank is unit, frail fraction, fault we fill
with sever-augur, failing into new
blame-blooms, pain-rhumes, contusions. Make it ill.

This ellipse, slip between seasons,
a concatenation of leaves
twisting themselves in shrill sheaves
of shrivel, the rust-gray reasons

for teardrops scoring their lesions
in every substance that grieves—
and the dreaming sleeper believes,
mistress of palest collisions,

she masters the tender elisions
of eye and why and night—and bliss
(overblooming its cause) will whirl

the spring-and-autumn integral
and wide the green dying that is
black blood of whitest precisions.

Yet, though. No one speaking, no one moves,
no one asking how the something was,
or why the what was wondered (just because)
or how the x was augured, how it proves

the erring atomy contingent loves
crux on minus—the set, transparent jaws,
tintinnabula of pewter paws
nicking and pacing. A specter stalks the roofs,

nothing is wanting. Nothing in its frame
gives the nascencies a colder name;
the body-midwife with its semblant gloves

delivers the zero-baby, self not same,
a skeleton-child, a discordant rhyme,
effulgent dissonance of metal doves.

The day-slate, erasing. Day shades into mist,
a graying peering, a graspless plain
ceding line to blur, figure to stain,
a dimming drowsing no substance can resist.

A mineral sifting, shale-whorl or schist
that day the miner splits in flinting rain,
a breathing solid—air-ore—metallic grain,
many-bodied, nothing-boundaried, million-kissed

numinous rumor, edgeless and rent
in silver increments, shivering, to shift
water to air to earth to warmth to pure

motile stasis, like a whole veil, demure
infant-body, earth-nimbus, palest rift
and margin's minion—the whispered element.

What is this witness, the watching ages,
yield of hours, blurred nights, the blue commerce
limned limpidities the skies rehearse
dreaming their seasons, raptured in their rages.

Eventless auction the sun screams and stages
for outered spectacles that bloom their source,
or eyes are mouths and utter tongued remorse—
read me, augur, from the wrists of sages

the shocks and tangencies strangled in their veins.
Or stars are livid links in lucent chains.
Heart will read its figure in its willing

or blinded needle the compass stains;
lidless volumes and vortices of pains
distinct the dolor, and kind the killing.

Nice knuckle, uncle. Nice hat, hornet.
Nice is nervouser than eye or at,
the gone get going, the icons eat
a lawful loin, an iridescent sweet

glows its grid-iris, the noun forget.
Pliez! keep folding, administer the that,
perennials languished in a pliant heat
stay go come stay, white nunca, red meat—

green is the color of time or *green is gram*
or *green as mold is the house of oblivion*
and green how I want you green, that house of am

loves its numberables, the lamping sham—
quick candle, click the trigger in the tun,
red now, green when, that shocks the shaking sun.

The blue blanched figures—system of bird—
possess the future in the singing spring,
syrinx opulens, the eye a ring
noon will burn in like a perfect word

in a breathing sentence the silence blurred.
Principally throat, motion arriving
aural integral or static wing
comes to this remonstrance, harm, high, heard

and white kept opiate the nothing wides.
Palliative the skewed sky shackles, flails.
High integument that curts and glides

and beads the waters where its silver sails
the streaming numbers, aureate scales.
Enough says the girl and screams and hides.

I asked every flower I met
had they seen my palest friend.
The chant of the roots will beget
petals that blazon and bend

and erasable eyes to forget
the sun and the storm and the wind,
the sky which wheels in its net,
the black of the blurrest portend.

"We see in the sheerest clair
the nothing that vitals and vides.
No friend of your night and your debt

will blight our murmur with seeds
of the mortal flower, regret,
which roots in the arc of the air."

Gray airs, gray stirs. A form of flesh
nets its gray catch. The system swims.
Shibboleth synth, stanchions symptoms
effervescing to relinquish

rectilinears of rush and ash.
Gray gris, grau day, grisaille of sums,
gristle granular of stateless kingdoms,
spore and structure still distinguish

ghosts in spokes—the features flash,
the futures silver—spiral spumes
oceans of errata, columns

stutter, gray pearls that were his crash,
or fallow hull—grayness blooms
the no-wind its nightlessness consumes.

Now you nerve. Flurred, avid as the raw
worm in the bird's throat. It weirds the song.
The *day die darkly* in the ear all wrong—
all wreck, all riot—the maiden spins the straw,

the forest falters. Night is what she saw,
in opaque increments deafening the tongue.
Sleep bird, sleep body that the silence strung,
myrrh-moon, bright maudlin, weeping as you draw

white tears, pearl iris in a net of eyes.
The spinning maiden quickens her design.
Gold gut spooling, integument of awe,

a baby breathing as a bird is wise
(the bird-bright heart that flutters like a law)
which eats the excess. The strangle in the shine.

Dull wheel
shall stall
ordeal
appall

still peal
whole wall
or rill
a call

a keel
will hull
until

a rule
a cruel
annul

Reticulation of a premise
emerges in even harm
volitional as a storm
or stanching of plot and promise.

Latencies—the loss, the minus—
consider the song of the worm:
"am sightless as wing, leg, arm,
under my raw seeps the rawness."

How does a namelessness name?
Suppose it were better off dead.
Or its tongue were a species of beam

jouissance of the burning to seem
occult, aureate, aspect, thread,
not number that nevers the scheme.

II

Blank bride of the hour, occluded thought
wed to waning like a sifting scent
of future flowers, retrograde intent
backwards blooming as a nascent nought

staining minutes, rumorous, uncaught.
You callow hollow of the efferent,
the apsis-axis of my implement,
vague body, unboundaried, portionless plot

no chart remarks. My paltry pretty, go
blanch your blossoms (the radix of a rot)
in some white wind some nightness stanches, stale

negative lumen of a spectral no.
What center cinches your orbit's knot,
the far aphelion of a darkest veil?

The throat-flute uttering its constant note
of claim and name and wake and never-same
and nuanced cadences of sate, remote
days translated into a breathing frame,

knows its viewless voice is future's lend,
surpassing present where it grows and dwells
momently, glancing vocable, to spend
blooming fullness as it spills and swells

in the air ear, othered. Heard, is it the same?
Future-fathered, present-mothered—instrument
of mute contingencies its songs declaim

note by note by stopless increment
in the sounding, silenced. Audible degree
nights the note that lets mind's nighttime see.

To ruse and fuse, measured mortal
provisioned on plural delay
apportion the ardent decay
imprimatur dealt the detail

of sanguine or salt, the sable
division devising dismay.
Dies, sleeps, sweet salt, will or may
the mouth of the burnished bell

awake in a phonic torment
(arrest abort terminate)
as every howl is dormant

the figures illuminate.
Rise ruse round the golded door,
phase-fuse where the sleepers endure.

Show me the body that brides its quest,
that sleeps its seemings, tremblant inconnue,
jeweled Ophelia of diaphanous hue
in all her slippings, weed-wedded, water-dressed,

the sluice and swooning of her semblant rest—
the river ruptures, the weeds branch blue—
day's jaune eyes (wide lucencies) bleed new
hollow spaces where the breathings nest,

irised mnemosyne, rumored as a rune.
Oh roared red pulse, errata, when you die
maiden-postured, murmur in the wrist,

tendrilled syllables the waters twist,
or innered element (it is an I)
the dead girl blurring in the blooded noon.

Red petal digits. The stone day stalls.
Ceremonial as a private pride,
cold swifts stitch patterns that the winds elide,
transparent ornaments a thought appalls

arabesquing in its cogent walls,
axial furor, nomen in the glide.
Is it the scar of figure, gaping wide,
that webs wet wings and veins the tinny calls,

the bird-blue wound flowered as a fear,
replication of the carbon tear
the figure-birds devour? Blue boundaries sing

Border is the number of each thing,
scoring the sever, static in the ear,
fallow nominal of a touchless near.

When ash November orders its demise
and something hollow hovers in the trees
yawning yellow, sallow auguries
sowing numbness in the zero skies

and wind grows brittle, scudded, gray surmise
of no one's question, nothing's start or cease
or let or wait, no voice's *no* or *please*
sifting minutes clicking—the palest eyes

close and that pale planet, killing need
kills the orbit where the icons curve,
transparent coordinates, factored seed

and stars, and shapes erasing—static swerve
of figures stuttered—bloodless spaces bleed
each human cutting, vertebrae and nerve.

I asked every flower I met
had they seen my palest friend.
The one called world-without-end
shook from its august arrête.

"A blink in the dark, pauvrette,
this business of breach and mend."
Then to search is only to spend?
A bier in the air, oubliette?

"Fertility's fraud is forget.
The soil that strains in the eye
breeding *nuance, nascence, name*

re-blooming a world that will die.
Each grain is a doorless *my*.
To search is only to same."

One says none is nascent, noon is due
when two's bleak blinded hybrid twins the light.
None says no one numbers less than two,
the one who days, the one who darks all night.

Noon's cold name is cloven, frigid height,
a one-division in the random, fault
split in fusion's faction, no one's bright
eyeless acme arcing—cohesive vault.

That one were none's skulled infant, second sight
of two's twained woes, and tangled toxic root,
nearer to nothing, nameless, sequent blight,

as two's black ruse slits mind a riven fruit.
These sumless parents, two and null, make one
Queen of Quotient, who adds her x to none.

Tilt the placeless waver of this moving
over the wanton waters—spiral storm
hates the harmonies the days conform,
orage orgueil, an intenser proving

lashing its vassals, a form of loving.
Dolor, choler, how the moods deform
this ruse of light red rudiments perform—
horse and horse, fox fox, fast flick and fauving,

emblems in their leap and scrap, the livid nerving
worlds consume, design, and name a grieving.
Your impenitent animal: sky-pelt,

net and gnaw, and claw and fleet and swerving;
day's raw quiddities that roar a leaving;
eye-gold arrows, pierce-pulse; a failing felt.

Lease of my leaving, heartfelt lack, what does
your plunge propose, its too-loose turning?
A deepfall trill, always-again returning
when Leaving, stepchild of Staying, is and was

always already going, condition, cause
of future's rapture—the baby always burning—
and present never present, always yearning
for plummet's pivot—articulate pause.

Lack lurks, blue and black. What acrid, airy sea
will give the whither anchor, heed the calling
for harbor, shore, to stall the listing lee

of always-motion, infant and appalling?
My infinite late, dark nascence: Tell me,
will there be an end to all this falling?

The pearl of interval, the still of yet,
poises momently, balancing the bend
and wave, slip, slope, and sine the seconds send
vertiginous minutes, airy with forget,

pale with height. The pause-pearl jewels the net,
an aleph-iris callowing portend
as though the present were its livid end
and blanch the blink that dazzles every debt.

It is its instant. Perfect circle, skull.
Bliss in statis, suspension at the swell;
interiority of gaze that frames

and fixes, finishes, the flux of names;
the hull the stall, effulgent—scale and shell
and opal effigy, adequate of null.

Sign or cipher paints the green bird green.
Wipe the wet outer of the eye, the white.
They say: "it's dawn." Morning eats the night.
Morrow multiple, and worlds between,

and stagnant waters reeking in their sheen.
View this. And do. The harrow in the heat,
the tongue that spills its supple tender meat.
The mood machine will click cerulean

systems into spasms, a care elate;
specificity or stuttered plot.
It is no silence that the bliss-birds blight.

Or night-notes failing, humming weed or wait.
Cache cache, sing the figures, the weep is what
nerves their wire whirring, to ignite.

Retinal snowfall, anything that slips,
where children kick a snowman in the dim
winter increment, the gray of 3 PM.
Two red cars, one blue. White wing that dips

and opens softly in the eyes' ellipse,
an n dimension furling at the rim—
a down is paling—shyer motions limn,
shyest motions adumbrate the tips—

the edges ether, falter. World will be
reconstituted as an airy scree—
white waif particles, a haze of eyes,

meticulous slippings, data from the skies.
Oh angry kids, the semblance you don't see
dissembles also. Kill it where it lies.

See the crack at the quick of accident?
Day's transparencies and light that twins
its farthest falling with a rising scent
of roots—dark, rumorous—whose reach begins

repleted sequences of meaning spent
on fetid fruits, encased in ruptured skins.
The Scar Hypothesis—a theory meant
to stitch divisibles, the fruitful sins

of cultivated conscience. If the proof—
bluest sutures in the blackest slit—
won't round the fruit (pale flesh and paler rind),

to some hale wholeness, oval and aloof,
what grounds unearth, what propositions split
disfigured orders accident designed?

Intoxicant ferment of a pale alcool
stains the fragrance of a stranger tongue
and blurs the silence it was born among.
The sallow Fate is sighing to her spool,

Fly on, pale days, where random is the rule
and loop the larynx where the throat is stung
by blind black bees whose wrath will spill unsung
and night will eat the sweet, the onyx jewel,

the hive-sieve drowning in its fallow shell.
The sky-stung bees bloom velvet as a bell,
gnawing and churring like a dream of eyes

longing to swallow the substance they can feel.
The Fate has slit the coil on the wheel.
The blue blade shudders where the honey dries.

That's what it says to the bloomingest more,
don't ask the reason, follow the plume
to its fullest expression, the blood-burnt room
bleeding its name, autonomous ore

mining the season it was plundered for.
These and those, blurred tether, blond écume
sky intransigent of passage, rude loom
coiled and cabled, polyphonous store

sounding its seemings. Apple, atom, eye,
crux of nuance, manifest of why,
shall there be shale and hollow, fix and list,

a zero mattered, a quiescence kissed,
rouge reine who rules the wrack and motley mien
the rain of faces, flesh-figured, dead green.

The thing you do you keep or claim—
there was this reason, scattered squall
blurring its faces, random thrall
of crones and clones, replicate same

shatters its single, riven name.
Oh holy puppet, genius doll,
we like to touch it, call it all
the shunt of heartwork, lurid fame

some lucent lady cradles close,
and smiling, dimming, speaks one thin
immanent syllable, viral rose

hissing its petals, ciphered skin
no word will bleed, no wound you chose
deeps the speaking its noons begin.

A premise, a solace—deciduous dress.
A figment garment, ornament of leaves
that tip and trill and flail, kinetic sleeves
and skirt of scatter, skirting autumn's less.

Pale-slow, slow-pale. Console the maiden, bless
her fraying figure, attenuating eves
and pale slow days when a sapped sun grays and grieves
and moon's pale plummet plurals, passionless.

Arboreal time. Bone time. Marrow grows
and wakeful, wakes its ages, and decrees
blinding doctrines, darking—fragmented snows

seeping to sources, as a bright eye will close
in a night room, sightless. Lovers turn to trees,
trees to lovers. And each gown shreds and glows.

She goes, she is, she wakes the waters
primed in their wave-form, a flux of urge
struck into oneness, the solid surge
seeking completion, and strikes and shatters

and is its fragments, distinction's daughters—
and now, unholding, the cleave and merge
the hew and fusing, plundering the verge
and substance is the scheme it scatters

and what it numbers in substantial sun.
Her hands hold many or her hands hold none.
And diving the salt will kiss a convex eye

and be salt fact and be the bodied sky
and that gray weight is both or beggared one,
a dead dimensional, or blue begun.

The needs that propagate the handful, them,
in all their tiny bleatings in the case
make noon a noun imperatives erase,
the garish gown unravelled at the hem,

the cool carnation havocked from the stem.
How come you knew no better, bleeding face?
You took, you broke, circumference a base
ampling all the bodies of the whim.

These are the artfullest beings, all their beams
make blank night a seance of extremes—
candle craves inferno, conic egg

sallows its embryo, to blurt, to beg
blaze in cadences of raptured streams—
and all etcetera strangles in its seams.

All the things unbluing: skies erase
actual ether, a trace a whole could tell
to keep its edges tender, tangible
stammer and falter. Sere-saturate. A race

is the pure recrimination of time to space
and slits the sun (scar-seed that splits a shell)
and drips its minutes, and tides a ticking swell,
lucent liquid drowning to fluoresce

the skirl of radial. It clicks. It was.
It seeps, accretes. Squalls, plurals. Blooms a bell—
cold notes, cold audibles, as silence does

fulgurance, calculus. If *final* fell—
illuminata of the palest pause—
would time annul the zero in the laws?

Bitter seed—scarred semblance—Psyche
sows the portion of contagion, liberty
in nerve and number, Cupid's quiddity
who catalogues the adage, zed to z,

and spends the nothing lovers' numbing plea
It shall be if we kiss it. Stone can see
what factors fault its fathoms, ardor we
mistake for fracture. A split, a volt, a v

of vain misgiving, void's elected *be*
knowing no rapture but its own redundancy.
So vowels do not die. They scale and scree

and haunt the planets with a harmony
as the zodiac wheels its pale menagerie
of soundless animals no love can free.

This din and this condition. Thinking thief
who nicks and strips and skitters all away
as conscious night will dark a callow day
and make a woe a weal. Is pain belief,

wilder slivers in a broken leaf
that falls and fades and fails, until they say
who thought this shred could measure, scrap could weigh
vacant volumes on a scale of grief.

Din and yammer. The noise is in the quick,
the sentient sap that wells, the quern of now
milling its tears. Sweet sentence, what will stay

of all this wayless weeping, as the sick
tear-shaped leaves slip, whisper, news of how
silence whitens every bright array.

It is not a question of the will, this one.
Or call it magnetic tape, *musique concrète.*
There is not enough of nothing in it.
One's intended actions in relation

with the ambient unintended ones
the sounds of the knives and the forks, the street
noises—furniture music—not just the discrete
chosen conventions, the common

denominator is zero, where the heart beats.
Otherwise the music will need walls to defend
itself—no one *means* to circulate

his blood—walls which will not only constantly be in
need of repair, but which even
to get a drink of water, we must pass beyond.

Nothing was ever what it claimed to be,
the earth, blue egg, in its seeping shell
dispensing damage like a hollow hell
inchling weeping for a minor sea

ticking its tidelets, x and y and z.
The blue beneficence we call and spell
and call blue heaven, the whiteblue well
of constant waters, deepening a thee,

a thou and who, touching every what—
and in the *or*, a shudder in the cut—
and that you are, blue mirror, only stare

bluest blankness, whether in the where,
sheen that bleeds blue beauty we are taught
drowns and booms and vowels. I will not.

Lifting whither, cycle of the sift
annuls the future, zero that you zoom
beautiful suitor of the lucent room
evacuating auras, stratal shift

leaping in its alabaster rift.
Lend the daylight crescent, circle, spume,
ether from your eye, appalled perfume,
ash incense to boundary when you drift

bluely looming—motion will be mute
season spooling its argent errant thread
endless loop and lavish as the dead

note resounding a transparent flute.
Tell the boys we're leaving—wind as red
event left at the altar—the bride is fled.

Acknowledgments

My deepest thanks to the friends who have read and encouraged these poems these years. And to my colleagues and students at the University of Montana for their generosity, sweetness, and wit.

Grateful acknowledgment to the editors who have published these poems in the following journals: *American Letters and Commentary, Boston Review, Canary, Chicago Review, Columbia: A Journal of Literature and Art, Crowd, Denver Quarterly, Electronic Poetry Review, Gulf Coast, New American Writing, New England Review, NC3, No Journal, Octopus, Parakeet, Paris Review, Ploughshares, Slope, Sonora Review,* and *Verse.*

And in these anthologies:

American Poets in the 21st Century: The New Poetics, Claudia Rankine and Lisa Sewell, Editors. Middletown, CT: Wesleyan University Press, 2007.

The Gertrude Stein Awards in Innovative Poetry, Douglas Messerli, Editor. Los Angeles: Green Integer Press, 2008.

The Iowa Anthology of New American Poetries, Reginald Shepherd, Editor. Iowa City: University of Iowa Press, 2005.

Long Journey: Contemporary Northwest Poets, David Biespiel, Editor. Corvallis, OR: Oregon State University Press, 2006.

Poems Across the Big Sky: An Anthology of Montana Poets, Lowell Jaeger, Editor. Kallispell, MT: Many Voices Press, 2007.

The Pushcart Prize Anthology XXVI, Bill Henderson, Editor. Wainscott, New York: Pushcart Press, 2002. Reprinted in *The Pushcart Book of Poetry,* Joan Murray, Editor. 2006.

Sad Little Breathings & Other Acts of Ventriloquism, Heather McHugh, Editor. Seattle: Publishing Online, Inc., 2002.

Under the Rock Umbrella: Contemporary American Poets from 1951–1977, William Walsh, Editor. Macon: Mercer University Press, 2006.

Thanks too to the Fundación Valparaíso in Mojacar, Spain, where some of these poems were written.

Epigraph: Gilles Deleuze, from *The Logic of Sense*, Tr. Mark Lester. New York: Columbia University Press, 1990.

"It is not a question of the will" is composed of phrases from John Cage's "Erik Satie," in *Silence*. Hanover, NH: Wesleyan University Press, 1961.

About the Author

Karen Volkman is the author of *Crash's Law* (Norton, 1996), a National Poetry Series selection, and *Spar* (University of Iowa Press, 2002), which received the Iowa Poetry Prize and the James Laughlin Award from the Academy of American Poets. Her poems have appeared in numerous anthologies, including *The Best American Poetry*, *The Pushcart Prize Anthology*, *American Poets in the 21ˢᵗ Century: The New Poetics*, and *The Gertrude Stein Awards in Innovative Poetry*. Recipient of awards from the NEA, the Poetry Society of America, Akademie Schloss Solitude, and the Bogliasco Foundation, she has taught at several universities, including the University of Alabama, University of Pittsburgh, University of Chicago, and Columbia College Chicago. She currently lives in Missoula and teaches at the University of Montana.

BOA Editions, Ltd.
American Poets Continuum Series

Nomina, sonnets by Karen Volkman, is set in Linotype Didot, a font based on types cut by Firman Didot in Paris in 1783; it is characterized by abrupt changes from thick to thin strokes and hairline serifs.

The publication of this book is made possible, in part, by the special support of the following individuals:

Anonymous (2)
Kazim Ali
Angela Bonazinga & Catherine Lewis
Alan & Nancy Cameros
Gwen & Gary Conners
Peter & Sue Durant
Pete & Bev French
Dane & Judy Gordon
Kip & Debby Hale
Peter & Robin Hursh
Willy & Bob Hursh
X. J. & Dorothy M. Kennedy
Laurie Kutchins
Jack & Gail Langerak
Rosemary & Lewis Lloyd
James Logenbach & Joanna Scott
Irving Malin
Boo Poulin
Roland Ricker
Steven O. Russell & Phyllis Rifkin-Russell
Vicki & Richard Schwartz
Thomas R. Ward
Patricia D. Ward-Baker
Pat & Mike Wilder
Glenn & Helen William